Remote Work

Revolution:

"Transforming Careers and Job Opportunities"

Willie A. Wright

Contents

The Evolution of Remote Work:

From Necessity to Preference

"The Evolution of Remote Work: From Necessity to Preference" refers to the transition of remote work from being a necessity, driven by external factors such as pandemics or crises, to becoming a preferred mode of work for both employees and employers. This evolution has been accelerated by advancements in technology and changes in work culture, resulting in a significant shift in how and where work is conducted.

1. **Necessity of Remote Work:**
   The concept of remote work has been around for decades, primarily utilized by freelancers, consultants, and certain industries that allowed for

flexible work arrangements. However, the necessity of remote work gained prominence during global events such as the COVID-19 pandemic, which forced many businesses to adapt rapidly to remote work setups to ensure business continuity while minimizing health risks. During this phase, remote work was seen as a temporary solution to unforeseen challenges, and companies scrambled to provide their employees with the necessary tools and infrastructure to work from home effectively.

2. **Technological Advancements:** One of the key drivers behind the evolution of remote work was the continuous advancement of technology. High-speed internet, cloud computing, collaboration tools, and communication platforms have significantly improved the ability to work remotely. These technologies

have bridged the physical gap between employees and their workplaces, allowing them to collaborate seamlessly from different locations.

3. **Changing Work Culture and Employee Preferences:** As employees experienced remote work during the necessity phase, many realized its potential benefits. Work-life balance, reduced commuting time, and the ability to create a personalized workspace are some advantages that employees appreciated. This shift in work culture was further influenced by younger generations entering the workforce, who often prioritize flexibility and work-life integration over traditional office-based setups.

4. **Employer Perspectives:** Employers, too, began to recognize the advantages of remote work. Reduced

overhead costs associated with maintaining physical office spaces, access to a larger talent pool beyond geographical limitations, and increased productivity in certain cases became attractive incentives for businesses to adopt remote work policies.

5. **Flexibility as a Perk:**
   As remote work became more prevalent, it transformed from a mere necessity into a desirable perk for attracting and retaining talent. Many companies started offering remote work options as part of their benefits package to appeal to a broader range of candidates, and some even adopted fully remote or hybrid work models to provide flexibility while maintaining collaboration opportunities.

6. **Challenges and Adaptations:**
   Despite its benefits, remote work also posed challenges. Issues such as work-life balance, communication

barriers, feelings of isolation, and potential security risks needed to be addressed. As the trend evolved, companies started implementing various strategies to overcome these challenges. Regular virtual team meetings, team-building activities, digital communication norms, and cybersecurity measures became essential components of remote work adaptation.

7. A Hybrid Future:

As remote work evolved, it became evident that a one-size-fits-all approach might not be suitable for every company. While some businesses embraced fully remote work models, others opted for hybrid arrangements, combining remote and in-office work. The hybrid model sought to strike a balance between the advantages of remote work and the benefits of in-person collaboration.

In conclusion, "The Evolution of Remote Work: From Necessity to Preference" showcases how remote work, once driven by necessity, has transformed into a preferred way of working for many individuals and businesses. This transformation was enabled by technological advancements, changing work culture, and a growing understanding of the benefits and challenges of remote work. The future of work appears to be more flexible, with remote work likely to remain an integral part of the modern work landscape.

Advantages and Challenges of Remote Work for Employers and Employees

Remote work offers several advantages and challenges for both employers and employees. Let's delve into each aspect in detail:

Advantages of Remote Work for Employers:

1. **Cost Savings:** One of the most significant advantages for employers is cost savings. Remote work eliminates the need for large office spaces, reducing expenses associated with rent, utilities, and office supplies. Companies can redirect these funds to other areas of the business or invest in

employee development and well-being.

2. **Access to Global Talent:** Remote work allows employers to hire talent from around the world, breaking down geographical barriers. This expanded talent pool increases the chances of finding highly skilled and specialized professionals, potentially leading to improved team performance and innovation.

3. **Increased Productivity:** Some studies suggest that remote workers can be more productive due to reduced distractions and the ability to create personalized work environments. Remote employees often experience fewer interruptions from colleagues and have more control over their schedules, leading to higher concentration and efficiency.

4. **Employee Retention and Satisfaction:** Offering remote work options can enhance employee satisfaction and contribute to higher retention rates. Employees value the flexibility and work-life balance remote work provides, leading to increased job satisfaction and a stronger commitment to the organization.

5. **Business Continuity:** Remote work proved crucial during times of crisis, such as the COVID-19 pandemic. Having remote work capabilities ensures business continuity even during unforeseen circumstances, mitigating potential disruptions to operations.

Challenges of Remote Work for Employers:

1. **Communication and Collaboration:** Remote work can create communication challenges,

hindering spontaneous interactions and face-to-face collaboration. Employers must invest in digital communication tools and establish clear communication protocols to ensure effective team collaboration.

2. **Monitoring and Accountability:** Employers may find it challenging to monitor remote employees' performance and ensure they remain accountable. Implementing performance metrics and regular check-ins can help address this concern and maintain productivity levels.

3. **Cybersecurity Risks:** With remote work comes an increased risk of cybersecurity breaches. Employees accessing sensitive company data from personal devices or unsecured networks can expose businesses to potential security threats. Employers

need to invest in robust cybersecurity measures and educate employees about best practices.

Advantages of Remote Work for Employees:

1. **Flexibility and Work-Life Balance:** Remote work offers employees the flexibility to create a work schedule that accommodates their personal commitments, leading to improved work-life balance. This flexibility can contribute to reduced stress and increased overall well-being.

2. **Commute Elimination:** Remote work eliminates the need for daily commutes, saving employees valuable time and money. This reduction in commuting-related stress can lead to higher job satisfaction and improved mental health.

3. **Customized Work Environment:** Remote workers have the freedom to design their workspaces according to their preferences, resulting in a more comfortable and personalized working environment.

4. **Access to Job Opportunities:** Remote work allows employees to access job opportunities outside their immediate geographic area. This expanded job market can open up possibilities for career growth and development.

Challenges of Remote Work for Employees:

1. **Isolation and Loneliness:** Working remotely can lead to feelings of isolation and loneliness, as employees miss out on in-person interactions with colleagues. This can affect employee morale and may require

proactive efforts to foster team camaraderie through virtual team-building activities.

2. **Technology and Connectivity Issues:** Remote workers heavily rely on technology, and technical difficulties can disrupt their productivity. Employees need access to reliable internet connections and suitable hardware to perform their tasks efficiently.

3. **Blurred Work-Life Boundaries:** The flexibility of remote work can blur the boundaries between work and personal life, leading to potential burnout. Setting clear boundaries and adhering to a designated work schedule is crucial to avoid overworking.

4. **Career Growth and Networking:** Remote employees may find it more

challenging to build professional networks and access certain career development opportunities that are typically available in office settings.

In conclusion, remote work offers numerous advantages for both employers and employees, such as cost savings, increased productivity, and improved work-life balance. However, it also presents challenges related to communication, accountability, cybersecurity, and the potential for feelings of isolation. Successful implementation of remote work requires proactive measures to address these challenges and capitalize on the benefits remote work brings to the table.

Digital Nomadism:

A New Way of Work and Travel

Digital nomadism is a modern lifestyle that allows individuals to work remotely while traveling and living in different locations. Digital nomads use technology to perform their job duties, allowing them the freedom to choose their work environment, often opting for diverse and exotic destinations. This way of work and travel has gained popularity in recent years, driven by advancements in technology, changing work cultures, and a desire for more freedom and flexibility.

1. **Technology Empowerment:**
   Digital nomadism is made possible by the increasing accessibility of technology. High-speed internet, cloud computing, communication tools, and project management

software enable individuals to work effectively from anywhere in the world. Laptops, smartphones, and other portable devices serve as the essential tools for digital nomads, allowing them to stay connected with colleagues and clients while on the move.

2. **Flexibility and Freedom:**
One of the primary reasons people choose the digital nomad lifestyle is the freedom it offers. Nomads can determine their work hours and locations, allowing them to balance work commitments with personal interests and exploration. This flexibility enables them to choose when and where they work, making it easier to pursue hobbies, spend time with loved ones, and explore new cultures and places.

3. **Work-Life Integration:**
Digital nomads often blend their work and personal lives seamlessly. With the ability to work from cafes, co-working spaces, or scenic locations,

they can combine their professional responsibilities with leisure activities and travel experiences. This work-life integration can lead to increased job satisfaction and overall well-being.

4. **Diverse Cultural Experiences:** Digital nomadism allows individuals to immerse themselves in various cultures and experience life from different perspectives. By living in different locations, nomads have the opportunity to learn languages, try local cuisines, and engage with diverse communities, contributing to personal growth and global awareness.

5. **Networking Opportunities:** While traveling and working remotely, digital nomads have the chance to build a global network of like-minded individuals. They often connect with other nomads, entrepreneurs, and professionals through co-working spaces, online communities, and networking events. These connections can lead to collaborations,

partnerships, and potential business opportunities.

6. Cost Considerations:

Digital nomads can take advantage of cost discrepancies between different locations. They may choose to live in countries with a lower cost of living, stretching their budget while still maintaining a high quality of life. This financial flexibility can make it easier to explore new destinations and enjoy unique experiences.

Challenges of Digital Nomadism:

1. **Internet Reliability:** While technology enables digital nomadism, it also brings challenges. Reliance on stable internet connections is crucial for remote work, and not all destinations offer consistent and reliable internet access.

2. **Time Zone Differences:** Coordinating work with colleagues or clients across various time zones can be challenging, leading to potential

scheduling conflicts and communication delays.

3. **Work-Life Boundaries:** Maintaining a healthy work-life balance can be difficult for digital nomads. The lack of clear boundaries between work and leisure time may result in overworking or feeling disconnected from loved ones.

4. **Visa and Legal Issues:** Some countries have specific visa regulations that may not cater to digital nomads. Obtaining the right visas and navigating legal complexities can be time-consuming and stressful.

5. **Loneliness and Social Isolation:** Constantly changing locations can lead to feelings of loneliness and isolation, as digital nomads might not have a stable social circle or support network in each place they visit.

6. **Limited Job Opportunities:** Not all professions are easily adaptable to remote work, which limits the pool of

individuals who can embrace the digital nomad lifestyle. Certain industries and roles require physical presence or equipment not easily transportable.

In conclusion, digital nomadism represents a new and exciting way of work and travel, allowing individuals to leverage technology for remote work while exploring different parts of the world. The lifestyle offers freedom, flexibility, and diverse cultural experiences, but it also comes with challenges related to internet access, time zones, work-life boundaries, legal considerations, and social isolation. As the concept gains traction, more individuals and companies are exploring ways to embrace and accommodate this unique work-travel lifestyle.

Impact of Remote Work on Employee Productivity and Work-Life Balance

The impact of remote work on employee productivity and work-life balance has been a subject of significant interest, especially as remote work became more prevalent in recent years. Let's explore how remote work affects these aspects in detail:

1. **Employee Productivity:**
   a. ***Flexibility and Autonomy:*** Remote work provides employees with the flexibility to set their work hours and create a personalized work environment. This autonomy can lead to increased productivity as employees can work during their

most productive hours and optimize their work setups to suit their preferences.

b. ***Reduced Commute and Distractions:*** Without the need to commute to the office, employees can save valuable time and energy. Additionally, remote work can reduce workplace distractions, leading to improved focus and concentration on tasks.

c. ***Access to Comfortable Workspaces:*** Employees can design their workspaces to maximize comfort and productivity. Whether it's a home office, a co-working space, or a favorite cafe, having the freedom to choose a conducive workspace can positively impact productivity.

d. ***Higher Job Satisfaction:*** Research has shown that employees who have the flexibility of remote work often report higher job satisfaction. This satisfaction can translate into increased motivation and productivity.

2. **Work-Life Balance:**
    a. ***Flexible Schedules:*** Remote work allows employees to better balance work commitments with personal responsibilities. They can accommodate family needs, personal errands, or other activities without sacrificing work commitments.

    b. ***Reduced Stress:*** The elimination of commuting and the ability to manage personal life alongside work can reduce overall stress levels for employees, contributing to a better work-life balance.

c. ***Family and Caregiving Responsibilities:*** Remote work can be particularly beneficial for employees with family or caregiving responsibilities. They can be present for their families while still fulfilling work obligations.

d. ***Enhanced Well-being:*** A better work-life balance can lead to improved physical and mental well-being. Employees can have more time for relaxation, exercise, and hobbies, resulting in a healthier and happier workforce.

3. **Potential Challenges:** While remote work offers many benefits for productivity and work-life balance, it also presents some challenges:

a. ***Blurred Boundaries:*** Remote work can blur the lines between work and personal life, making it challenging for employees to switch off from work and fully disconnect during non-working hours.

b. ***Communication and Collaboration:*** Remote work can sometimes lead to communication challenges, especially when team members are dispersed across different locations. Effective communication tools and practices are essential to maintain collaboration and team cohesion.

c. ***Social Isolation:*** Employees working remotely may experience feelings of isolation and loneliness, especially if they lack regular in-person interactions with colleagues. Building and maintaining strong virtual team relationships is crucial to address this challenge.

d. ***Overworking:*** Some remote employees may struggle to set clear boundaries between work and personal time, leading to overworking and potential burnout. Employers should encourage employees to take breaks and establish healthy work habits.

e. ***Dependence on Technology:*** Technical issues or internet disruptions can hinder productivity and cause frustration for remote workers. Ensuring access to reliable technology and support is essential.

Remote work can significantly impact employee productivity and work-life balance positively when implemented thoughtfully. The flexibility, autonomy, and reduced stress associated with remote work can lead to increased productivity and a better work-life integration. However, it's crucial to address the challenges of blurred boundaries, communication, social isolation, and potential overworking to fully harness the benefits of remote work and ensure a healthy and engaged remote workforce. Employers must adopt effective remote work policies, provide necessary support, and prioritize employee well-being to make remote work a successful and sustainable arrangement.

The Role of Technology in Facilitating Remote Work

Technology plays a central and transformative role in facilitating remote work, enabling individuals and teams to collaborate effectively regardless of their physical locations. The integration of various technological tools and platforms has been instrumental in making remote work a viable and successful option for businesses and employees alike. Let's explore the key aspects of technology's role in facilitating remote work:

1. **Communication and Collaboration Tools:**
   a. ***Video Conferencing:*** Platforms like Zoom, Microsoft Teams, Google Meet, and others have revolutionized remote

communication. Video conferencing allows face-to-face interactions, team meetings, client presentations, and more, bridging the gap between remote team members.

b. ***Instant Messaging:*** Tools like Slack, Microsoft Teams, and others facilitate real-time chat and quick communication among team members. These platforms enhance collaboration, enabling seamless sharing of ideas and information.

c. ***Email and Cloud Storage:*** Email remains an essential means of communication, allowing for formal messages and file sharing. Additionally, cloud storage services like Google Drive, Dropbox, and

OneDrive provide a centralized space for storing and sharing documents, ensuring easy access for remote teams.

2. **Project Management and Task Tracking:**
   a. ***Project Management Software:*** Tools such as Asana, Trello, and Jira help remote teams organize tasks, set deadlines, and track project progress. These platforms enhance team coordination and ensure that everyone is on the same page regarding project milestones and deliverables.

   b. ***Time Tracking Software:*** Time tracking tools assist in monitoring and managing remote employees' work hours, ensuring accurate invoicing, and helping employees stay accountable for their time and tasks.

3. Virtual Collaboration Platforms:

a. ***Virtual Whiteboards:*** Virtual whiteboard tools like Miro and MURAL allow teams to brainstorm, collaborate on ideas, and visualize projects in a digital workspace, simulating the experience of an in-person whiteboard session.

b. ***Virtual Team-Building Activities:*** Various platforms offer virtual team-building activities to foster team bonding and camaraderie among remote employees.

4. Cybersecurity and Data Protection:

a. ***Virtual Private Networks (VPNs):*** Remote work often requires employees to access company data and systems from external networks. VPNs encrypt internet connections, enhancing security and protecting sensitive information.

b. ***Endpoint Security:*** Endpoint security solutions safeguard remote devices, such as laptops and smartphones, from potential cyber threats and data breaches.

5. **Performance Monitoring and Analytics:**
   a. ***Employee Monitoring Software:*** Some companies use employee monitoring tools to track productivity and performance metrics. These tools can help identify areas for improvement and assess remote team members' contributions.

   b. ***Analytics and Reporting:*** Data analytics and reporting tools offer insights into team performance, project status, and overall productivity, enabling data-driven decision-making.

6. Training and Development:
a. ***Virtual Training Platforms:*** Remote work necessitates virtual training solutions to onboard new employees, conduct professional development workshops, and ensure continuous learning within the organization.

Overall, technology plays a pivotal role in facilitating remote work by providing the infrastructure for seamless communication, collaboration, and data management. As remote work becomes more common, businesses will continue to leverage innovative technological solutions to optimize remote team performance and foster a dynamic and productive virtual work environment. It's essential for organizations to invest in reliable and secure technology and provide adequate training and support to ensure a successful transition to remote work arrangements.

Redesigning Physical Workspaces for Hybrid Work Models

Redesigning physical workspaces for hybrid work models involves creating flexible and adaptable environments that cater to both in-office and remote employees. As businesses embrace hybrid work arrangements, where employees split their time between working in the office and remotely, it's essential to optimize physical spaces to support collaboration, productivity, and employee well-being. Here are some key considerations and strategies for redesigning physical workspaces for hybrid work models:

1. **Embrace Activity-Based Workspaces:**
   Activity-based workspaces offer different areas within the office

designed for specific tasks or activities. These spaces can include quiet zones for focused work, collaborative areas for team meetings, and social spaces for informal interactions. Creating a variety of work environments caters to the diverse needs of employees, whether they are working in the office or remotely.

2. Implement Flexible Seating Arrangements:

Flexible seating arrangements, such as hot-desking or unassigned seating, allow employees to choose their workstations based on their daily needs. This approach accommodates both in-office and remote employees who occasionally come to the office, promoting a sense of equality and ensuring that no one feels left out or without a designated workspace.

3. Optimize Technology Integration:

Ensure that the office spaces are equipped with technology that supports seamless collaboration between in-office and remote team members. High-quality video conferencing equipment, interactive whiteboards, and integrated communication tools enhance virtual meetings and foster effective communication between hybrid teams.

4. Focus on Ergonomics and Comfort:

Invest in ergonomic furniture and equipment to promote employee comfort and well-being. Proper seating, adjustable desks, and ergonomic accessories can contribute to the overall health and productivity of employees, regardless of where they work.

5. **Enhance Digital Accessibility:**
As hybrid work relies heavily on digital tools, ensure that all necessary documents, files, and resources are accessible to both in-office and remote employees. Cloud-based storage solutions and a centralized digital platform enable easy sharing and collaboration, reducing any disparities between physical and virtual team members.

6. **Create Collaboration Hubs:**
Designate specific areas within the office as collaboration hubs, where employees can gather for brainstorming sessions, team meetings, or project discussions. These spaces should be equipped with technology and tools that support effective collaboration, even when some team members participate remotely.

7. **Foster a Culture of Flexibility and Trust:**
   Redesigning physical workspaces for hybrid models is not just about the physical changes; it also involves fostering a culture of flexibility and trust. Encourage managers to focus on results rather than hours worked and create a culture that values output and contribution over physical presence.

8. **Offer Amenities and Wellness Spaces:**
   Provide amenities and wellness spaces that support employee well-being. Consider adding relaxation areas, quiet rooms, or outdoor spaces where employees can take breaks and recharge during their workday.

9. **Solicit Employee Feedback:**
   Involve employees in the redesign process by seeking their input and feedback. Conduct surveys, focus groups, or one-on-one discussions to understand their needs and

preferences, ensuring that the redesigned workspace aligns with their expectations.

10.   Monitor and Iterate:

Once the redesigned workspace is in use, regularly monitor its effectiveness and gather feedback from employees. Be open to making adjustments and improvements based on the evolving needs and preferences of the hybrid workforce.

In conclusion, redesigning physical workspaces for hybrid work models requires a thoughtful and holistic approach that prioritizes flexibility, collaboration, and employee well-being. By creating adaptable environments that accommodate both in-office and remote employees' needs, businesses can foster a cohesive and productive hybrid work culture that benefits everyone involved.

Virtual Collaboration Tools:

Enhancing Remote Teamwork and Communication

Virtual collaboration tools are essential software platforms that enable remote teams to communicate, collaborate, and work together effectively, regardless of their physical locations. These tools play a critical role in facilitating seamless virtual teamwork, ensuring smooth communication, and promoting productivity in remote work environments. Let's explore some of the most common virtual collaboration tools and their key features:

1. **Video Conferencing Platforms:** Video conferencing tools, such as Zoom, Microsoft Teams, Google Meet, and Webex, enable face-to-face virtual meetings. These platforms support real-time video and audio

communication, screen sharing, and chat features, making them ideal for team meetings, client presentations, training sessions, and one-on-one discussions.

Key Features:

- High-quality video and audio capabilities

- Screen sharing for presentations and demos

- Chat and messaging for real-time communication during meetings

- Integration with calendar and scheduling tools for easy meeting setup

2. Instant Messaging and Team Chat Apps:

Instant messaging platforms like Slack, Microsoft Teams, and Discord offer real-time chat capabilities, making it easy for team members to communicate and collaborate quickly. These tools allow for both one-on-one and group conversations, file sharing, and integration with other apps and services.

Key Features:

- Real-time chat for quick communication

- Channel-based organization for different teams and projects

- File sharing and integration with cloud storage platforms

- Notifications and alerts to keep teams updated on important messages

3. **Project Management Software:** Project management tools like Asana, Trello, and Monday.com help remote

teams organize tasks, track project progress, and collaborate on shared projects. These platforms provide visibility into project timelines, task assignments, and deadlines, ensuring that everyone is on the same page.

Key Features:

- Task tracking and assignment

- Project timelines and milestones

- Collaboration on project boards

- Integration with other productivity tools and communication platforms

4. **Cloud Storage and File Sharing:** Cloud storage services like Google Drive, Dropbox, and OneDrive allow remote teams to store and access files from anywhere with an internet connection. These platforms facilitate seamless file sharing and collaboration, reducing the need for emailing large attachments.

Key Features:

- Secure storage and backup of files in the cloud

- File sharing and permissions management

- Real-time collaboration on documents

- Version control to track changes in shared files

5. Virtual Whiteboard and Collaboration Spaces:
Virtual whiteboard tools like Miro and MURAL mimic physical whiteboards and allow remote teams to brainstorm, collaborate on ideas, and visualize projects together. These platforms enhance creativity and foster interactive collaboration.

Key Features:

- Digital whiteboard for brainstorming and ideation

- Templates for different types of projects and activities

- Real-time collaboration with remote team members

- Integration with other collaboration tools for seamless workflows

6. Task and Time Tracking Software:

Task and time tracking tools like Toggl and Harvest help remote employees monitor their work hours, track tasks, and manage time effectively. These tools assist in improving productivity, managing projects, and analyzing team performance.

Key Features:

- Time tracking for individual tasks and projects

- Reporting and analytics on time usage

- Integration with project management and communication tools

- Invoicing and billing functionalities for freelancers and consultants

In conclusion, virtual collaboration tools are instrumental in enhancing remote teamwork and communication. These platforms provide remote teams with the necessary infrastructure to collaborate seamlessly, share information, and work together effectively, regardless of geographical distances. By leveraging these tools, organizations can create a dynamic and productive remote work environment, fostering a sense of teamwork and cohesion among distributed team members.

Addressing Cybersecurity Concerns in a Remote Work Environment

Addressing cybersecurity concerns in a remote work environment is crucial to protect sensitive information, maintain data integrity, and safeguard against cyber threats. With remote work becoming more prevalent, ensuring robust cybersecurity measures is essential to mitigate potential risks. Let's explore in detail some of the key cybersecurity concerns in a remote work setup and the strategies to address them:

1. **Secure Remote Access:**
   Challenge: Providing remote employees with secure access to company resources and data without

compromising security is a top priority.

Solution:

- Implement Virtual Private Networks (VPNs) to encrypt internet connections and secure data transmission between remote devices and the company's network.

- Use multi-factor authentication (MFA) to add an extra layer of security, requiring users to provide additional verification factors when logging in.

- Ensure that all remote devices have updated security software, including firewalls and antivirus programs.

2. Data Protection and Privacy:
Challenge: Remote work can increase the risk of data breaches and

unauthorized access to sensitive information.

Solution:

- Enforce strict data access controls, limiting employee access to data based on their roles and responsibilities.

- Encrypt data at rest and in transit to protect sensitive information from unauthorized access.

- Implement data loss prevention (DLP) solutions to prevent the accidental or intentional leakage of confidential data.

3. Phishing and Social Engineering Attacks:

Challenge: Remote employees may be more susceptible to phishing attacks and social engineering scams due to potential distractions and unfamiliar surroundings.

Solution:

- Conduct regular cybersecurity training and awareness programs to educate employees about identifying and reporting phishing attempts.

- Use email security tools to detect and block phishing emails before they reach employees' inboxes.

- Encourage employees to verify suspicious requests through other communication channels before taking any action.

4. Endpoint Security:

Challenge: Remote devices, such as laptops and smartphones, may be more vulnerable to cyber threats, especially when used outside the company's secure network.

Solution:

- Require employees to use company-approved devices with up-to-date security software and configurations.

- Enable full-disk encryption on remote devices to protect data in case of theft or loss.

- Implement mobile device management (MDM) solutions to remotely monitor and secure employee devices.

5. Secure File Sharing and Collaboration:

Challenge: Remote teams need to collaborate and share files securely without risking data exposure or unauthorized access.

Solution:

- Use secure file-sharing platforms with access controls and encryption capabilities.

- Train employees on secure file-sharing practices and discourage the use of personal email accounts for work-related file transfers.

- Implement digital rights management (DRM) to control access to sensitive documents and prevent unauthorized sharing.

6. Secure Home Networks:

Challenge: Home networks may not have the same level of security as corporate networks, making them potential entry points for cyber attackers.

Solution:

- Encourage employees to secure their home Wi-Fi networks with strong passwords and WPA2 or WPA3 encryption.

- Provide guidelines for securing routers and updating firmware regularly.

- Consider offering employees home network security tools to protect against potential threats.

7. Incident Response and Reporting:

Challenge: Remote employees may not immediately report cybersecurity incidents, leading to delayed responses to potential threats.

Solution:
- Establish clear incident reporting procedures and channels for employees to report any cybersecurity incidents promptly.

- Conduct regular drills and simulations to test the incident response capabilities of remote teams.

- Provide employees with guidance on how to handle cybersecurity incidents and whom to contact in case of emergencies.

In conclusion, addressing cybersecurity concerns in a remote work environment requires a multi-layered approach that combines technical solutions, employee training, and proactive measures. By implementing strong security measures and fostering a cybersecurity-aware culture, organizations can minimize the risks associated with remote work and ensure the protection of sensitive data and systems.

Remote Work and the Future of Corporate Culture

Remote work has significantly impacted corporate culture and is poised to shape the future of how businesses operate and engage with their employees. The shift to remote work has accelerated cultural changes, creating new dynamics, challenges, and opportunities for organizations. Let's explore in detail how remote work influences corporate culture and its potential implications for the future:

1. **Flexibility and Work-Life Balance:**
   Remote work offers employees greater flexibility in managing their work schedules, which has a positive impact on work-life balance. As employees have more control over their time and

work environment, they experience reduced stress and better well-being. This shift towards work-life integration is likely to continue in the future, as employees increasingly prioritize flexibility and a healthy work-life balance.

2. Trust and Autonomy:

Remote work requires employers to trust their employees to deliver results without direct supervision. This trust-based approach fosters a culture of autonomy and empowers employees to take ownership of their work. As remote work becomes more common, the emphasis on trust and results-oriented management is expected to grow, redefining the traditional top-down management culture.

3. Communication and Collaboration:

Remote work necessitates efficient communication and collaboration tools to bridge the physical gap between team members. Organizations have adopted virtual communication platforms and digital collaboration spaces to foster teamwork and maintain a sense of connectivity. This emphasis on effective virtual communication is likely to remain integral to corporate culture, even in hybrid work environments.

4. Embracing Technology and Innovation:

The rapid transition to remote work accelerated the adoption of digital technologies and innovative tools to support remote collaboration. Companies have invested in virtual meeting platforms, project management software, and cloud-based tools. In the future, organizations are likely to continue leveraging technology to improve efficiency, creativity, and responsiveness.

5. **Inclusivity and Global Collaboration:**
Remote work breaks down geographical barriers and allows organizations to tap into a global talent pool. This inclusivity can enrich corporate culture by fostering diverse perspectives and experiences. In the future, businesses may prioritize diversity and global collaboration, leveraging remote work to create more inclusive and culturally rich work environments.

6. **Employee Engagement and Well-being:**
Maintaining employee engagement and well-being in a remote work setting is a critical challenge. Companies are adapting their culture to focus more on employee support,

mental health initiatives, and virtual team-building activities. In the future, successful corporate cultures will prioritize employee well-being to sustain a motivated and productive workforce.

7. **Redefining Office Spaces:**
As remote work becomes more prevalent, office spaces are likely to evolve. Companies may shift from traditional office setups to hybrid models, with office spaces serving as collaboration hubs rather than mandatory daily workspaces. The focus may be on providing spaces that foster creativity, innovation, and team bonding, while employees have the freedom to work remotely when needed.

8. **Continuous Learning and Skill Development:**
Remote work has highlighted the importance of continuous learning and skill development for employees

to stay competitive in a digital-first world. Organizations may invest more in remote training and development programs to equip employees with the skills necessary to thrive in remote and hybrid work environments.

In conclusion, remote work has already significantly impacted corporate culture, fostering flexibility, trust, and innovative approaches to work. The future of corporate culture is likely to revolve around a hybrid work model that emphasizes flexibility, inclusivity, employee well-being, and the effective use of technology. Organizations that embrace these changes and adapt their cultures accordingly are more likely to succeed in a rapidly evolving work landscape.

Remote Work and its Environmental Impact

Remote work has the potential to significantly impact the environment in both positive and negative ways. The shift towards remote work can lead to changes in energy consumption, transportation patterns, and resource utilization. Let's explore the environmental impact of remote work in detail:

Positive Environmental Impact:

1. **Reduced Greenhouse Gas Emissions:** One of the most significant environmental benefits of remote work is the reduction in greenhouse gas emissions. By eliminating or reducing daily commuting, remote work reduces the

use of fossil fuels in transportation, leading to lower carbon dioxide emissions and air pollution.

2. **Decreased Traffic Congestion:** With fewer employees commuting to centralized office spaces, traffic congestion is reduced, resulting in less idling and fuel consumption. This can lead to a reduction in air pollution and a decrease in the demand for road infrastructure.

3. **Energy Savings:** Remote work can lead to reduced energy consumption in office buildings. With fewer people using office spaces, there is a decrease in energy usage for lighting, heating, cooling, and other utilities, resulting in lower energy bills and a smaller carbon footprint.

4. **Conservation of Resources:** Remote work can contribute to the

conservation of resources, as less physical office space means reduced construction and maintenance requirements. Additionally, remote work often relies on digital communication and document sharing, reducing the need for paper and office supplies.

Negative Environmental Impact:

1. **Increased Home Energy Use:** While remote work reduces energy consumption in office buildings, it may increase energy usage at employees' homes. Additional electricity consumption from home offices, heating, and cooling can offset some of the environmental benefits of reduced office energy use.

2. **Digital Infrastructure:** The increased reliance on digital technology for remote work, including

servers and data centers, can lead to higher energy consumption in these facilities. The environmental impact of digital infrastructure depends on the energy sources used by data centers and cloud services.

3. **Electronic Waste:** The widespread use of technology for remote work can lead to an increase in electronic waste (e-waste). As employees upgrade their devices or rely on company-provided equipment, there is a need for responsible e-waste management and recycling practices.

4. **Reduced Public Transit Usage:** While remote work reduces individual car commuting, it may lead to reduced usage of public transportation. This could impact the financial viability of public transit systems, potentially reducing their accessibility and environmental benefits.

Overall, the environmental impact of remote work depends on several factors, including the energy sources in use, individual employee practices, and the extent to which remote work is embraced by organizations and individuals. To maximize the positive environmental impact of remote work, businesses and employees can take the following measures:

- Encourage the use of energy-efficient devices and appliances in home offices.

- Invest in renewable energy sources for home energy consumption and data centers.

- Promote responsible e-waste management and recycling.

- Encourage employees to adopt eco-friendly practices, such as using public transportation when commuting is necessary or reducing single-use items.

In conclusion, remote work has the potential to offer significant environmental benefits by reducing greenhouse gas emissions, traffic congestion, and resource consumption. However, it also poses challenges in terms of home energy use and the environmental impact of digital infrastructure. Balancing these factors and adopting eco-friendly practices can help organizations and employees maximize the positive environmental impact of remote work.

Inclusivity and Diversity in Remote Workforces

Inclusivity and diversity in remote workforces are critical aspects that promote a healthy and thriving work environment. Remote work has the potential to foster inclusivity and diversity by breaking down geographical barriers and enabling access to a broader talent pool. However, it also presents unique challenges that organizations must address to ensure that all employees feel valued, supported, and included. Let's explore in detail how inclusivity and diversity can be nurtured in remote workforces:

1. **Access to Global Talent:**
    Remote work allows organizations to hire talent from diverse geographic locations, increasing the potential for

a more inclusive and diverse workforce. By tapping into talent pools from different regions, cultures, and backgrounds, companies can enrich their teams with unique perspectives and skills.

2. **Flexible Work Arrangements:** Remote work offers employees greater flexibility in managing their work schedules, which can be especially beneficial for individuals with different needs and responsibilities. This flexibility can accommodate people with disabilities, caregivers, or those with other personal commitments, fostering an inclusive and supportive work environment.

3. **Emphasis on Inclusive Communication:** Remote work requires intentional efforts to ensure that communication is inclusive and accessible to all team

members. Companies should provide captioning and transcription services for virtual meetings, prioritize plain language in written communication, and encourage all team members to contribute their ideas and opinions.

4. Diverse Leadership Representation:

Promoting diversity and inclusivity starts with diverse leadership representation. Organizations should strive to create an inclusive culture that values and encourages diverse perspectives at all levels of the company. Having diverse leaders can foster a more inclusive work environment and serve as role models for employees from various backgrounds.

5. Cultural Sensitivity and Training:

Remote work can involve interactions with colleagues from different cultural backgrounds. Companies should provide training on cultural sensitivity and diversity to ensure that team members respect and understand each other's cultural norms and practices.

6. Inclusive Employee Resource Groups:

Establishing virtual Employee Resource Groups (ERGs) can be beneficial in fostering inclusivity and diversity in remote workforces. ERGs provide spaces for employees with shared backgrounds or experiences to connect, share experiences, and advocate for inclusivity within the organization.

7. Elimination of Unconscious Bias:

Organizations should remain vigilant about addressing unconscious bias in remote work settings. Implementing fair and transparent hiring practices, promoting diversity in job postings, and providing training on unconscious bias can help mitigate these issues.

8. Performance Evaluation and Recognition:

Ensure that performance evaluations and recognition are based on objective criteria and are free from bias. Recognize and celebrate the contributions of all team members, regardless of their location or background.

9. Regular Feedback and Employee Surveys:

Seek regular feedback from employees to understand their experiences in the remote work environment. Employee surveys can provide valuable insights into inclusivity and diversity challenges and opportunities.

10. **Mental Health and Well-being Support:**
Remote work can sometimes lead to feelings of isolation and loneliness. Companies should provide mental health support and resources to help employees navigate the challenges of remote work and maintain their well-being.

In conclusion, inclusivity and diversity are vital pillars of a successful remote workforce. Embracing remote work allows companies to access a broader talent pool, fostering a work environment that celebrates unique perspectives and experiences. However, it requires intentional efforts to address the challenges and barriers that remote work can create. By prioritizing inclusivity, cultural sensitivity, and diversity at all levels, organizations can build a thriving and cohesive remote workforce where all team members feel valued and empowered.

Government Policies and Regulations for Remote Work Arrangements

Government policies and regulations for remote work arrangements vary from country to country and can be influenced by factors such as labor laws, taxation, and social security systems. As remote work becomes more prevalent, governments are adapting their policies to address the unique challenges and opportunities presented by remote work. Let's explore in detail some of the key government policies and regulations related to remote work arrangements:

1. **Employment Contracts and Labor Laws:**
   Governments may have specific regulations governing remote work

contracts and agreements. These laws typically cover aspects such as working hours, overtime, rest periods, and minimum wage requirements. Employers must ensure that remote employees' contracts comply with the relevant labor laws and provide clear terms and conditions related to remote work arrangements.

2. Telecommuting Laws and Regulations:

Some countries have specific laws or guidelines related to telecommuting or remote work. These regulations may outline the rights and responsibilities of both employers and employees in remote work setups, including issues like data protection, health and safety standards for home offices, and employer-provided equipment.

3. Taxation and Social Security:

Remote work arrangements can have implications for taxation and social security contributions. Employees working in a different location than their employer's physical office may be subject to different tax rules. Governments may have specific guidelines on how to determine tax obligations for remote workers and their employers, considering factors such as the employee's location, the employer's location, and the nature of the work performed.

4. Work Visas and Residence Permits:

For international remote work arrangements, employees may need to obtain work visas or residence permits to work legally in a foreign country. Governments may have specific rules and requirements for remote workers who wish to work from abroad, and companies may need to navigate the complexities of immigration policies.

5. Data Protection and Privacy Laws:

Remote work often involves the transfer and storage of sensitive company and customer data. Governments may have data protection and privacy laws that require companies to take specific measures to safeguard data and ensure compliance with regulations when employees work remotely.

6. Occupational Health and Safety:

Occupational health and safety regulations apply to remote work environments just as they do in traditional workplaces. Governments may require employers to conduct risk assessments for home offices, provide ergonomic equipment, and ensure a safe working environment for remote employees.

7. Flexible Work Arrangements and Parental Leave:

Some governments have policies promoting flexible work arrangements, including remote work options, to support work-life balance for employees. Additionally, parental leave policies may be adapted to include provisions for remote working parents.

8. Collective Bargaining and Union Representation:

For employees represented by labor unions, remote work arrangements may be subject to collective bargaining agreements. Governments may have regulations outlining how remote work policies should be negotiated and implemented in unionized workplaces.

9. Training and Skill Development:

Governments may invest in training and skill development programs to equip workers with the necessary digital skills to succeed in remote work environments. These initiatives can enhance workforce readiness for remote work opportunities.

10.   **Monitoring and Enforcement:** Governments may establish mechanisms for monitoring and enforcing remote work policies and regulations to ensure that employers comply with the law and employees' rights are protected.

In conclusion, government policies and regulations for remote work arrangements are evolving to address the changing nature of work. As remote work becomes more widespread, governments are recognizing the need to provide clear guidelines and support to ensure fair, safe, and productive remote work environments for employees and employers alike. Organizations and remote workers should be aware of the specific policies and regulations that apply to their locations to ensure compliance and a positive remote work experience.

Balancing Flexibility and Accountability in Remote Work

Balancing flexibility and accountability in remote work is essential to create a productive and positive work environment. Remote work offers employees the freedom to manage their schedules and work from various locations, but it also requires a level of accountability to ensure that tasks are completed efficiently and that organizational goals are met. Let's explore in detail how organizations can strike the right balance between flexibility and accountability in remote work:

1. **Set Clear Expectations and Goals:**
   To foster accountability, it is crucial to establish clear expectations and goals for remote employees. Clearly

communicate the tasks, deadlines, and performance standards to ensure that everyone is on the same page. Having well-defined goals helps remote workers understand what is expected of them and provides a framework for measuring their progress and performance.

2. Empower Employees with Flexibility:

Flexibility is one of the significant advantages of remote work. Allow employees to have some control over their work schedules, as it can lead to increased job satisfaction and work-life balance. Giving employees the flexibility to choose their working hours, within reasonable limits, can lead to higher motivation and productivity.

3. Implement Outcome-Based Performance Metrics:

Move away from strict time-based tracking and focus on outcome-based performance metrics. Measure employee success based on the results they achieve rather than the number of hours they spend working. This approach allows employees to work at their most productive times and encourages them to focus on delivering quality results.

4. **Use Project Management and Collaboration Tools:** Implement project management and collaboration tools to track progress, allocate tasks, and foster transparency in remote work. These tools can help teams stay organized, communicate effectively, and share updates on project status, leading to increased accountability and efficiency.

5. **Encourage Regular Check-Ins and Communication:** Regular check-ins and communication are essential to ensure that remote

employees stay connected and receive the support they need. Managers should schedule one-on-one meetings, team calls, and virtual stand-ups to discuss progress, address challenges, and provide feedback. Open lines of communication contribute to accountability by enabling employees to seek help and guidance when needed.

6. **Provide Training and Development Opportunities:** Invest in training and development programs to help remote employees enhance their skills and knowledge. Providing opportunities for growth and learning can boost employee engagement and accountability, as employees feel more invested in their professional development.

7. **Foster a Culture of Trust:** Trust is the foundation of a successful remote work environment.

Demonstrate trust in your remote employees by giving them autonomy and ownership over their work. Trusting employees to manage their time and tasks can lead to a more accountable and engaged workforce.

8. Recognize and Reward Performance:

Recognize and reward employees who demonstrate accountability and achieve their goals. Positive reinforcement reinforces desired behaviors and motivates employees to continue delivering results.

9. Address Accountability Issues Proactively:

If accountability issues arise, address them proactively. Have candid conversations with employees to understand any challenges they may be facing and provide support or guidance to help them meet their responsibilities.

10. **Continuous Feedback and Performance Evaluation:** Regularly provide feedback and conduct performance evaluations to assess employee progress and align goals. Constructive feedback helps employees stay on track and make improvements as needed.

In conclusion, balancing flexibility and accountability in remote work requires a thoughtful and proactive approach. By setting clear expectations, empowering employees with flexibility, and implementing outcome-based performance metrics, organizations can foster a culture of accountability while reaping the benefits of remote work, such as increased productivity and employee satisfaction. Effective communication, trust-building, and ongoing support are essential to achieving this balance and creating a successful remote work environment.

Maintaining Work-Life Boundaries in a Remote Work Setup

Maintaining work-life boundaries in a remote work setup is crucial for ensuring employee well-being, productivity, and overall work-life balance. Remote work blurs the lines between work and personal life, making it essential for employees to establish clear boundaries to avoid burnout and maintain a healthy work-life integration. Here are some strategies for maintaining work-life boundaries in a remote work environment:

1. **Designate a Dedicated Workspace:** Create a designated workspace at home that is solely used for work-related activities. This helps

create a physical boundary between work and personal life, allowing you to mentally switch between the two when entering or leaving the workspace.

2. **Set Fixed Working Hours:** Establish specific working hours and communicate them to colleagues and family members. Adhering to a fixed schedule helps you create a clear separation between work hours and personal time.

3. **Create a Morning Routine:** Start your day with a morning routine that prepares you for work. This can include activities like exercise, meditation, or having a healthy breakfast. This routine helps signal the beginning of the workday and sets a positive tone for the day ahead.

4. **Take Regular Breaks:** Schedule regular breaks throughout the day to

rest and recharge. Stepping away from your workspace during breaks helps you mentally detach from work and maintain better focus when you return.

5. **Use a Timer for Work Tasks:** Use a timer or the Pomodoro technique to break your work into focused intervals with short breaks in between. This approach can help you stay productive during work hours and avoid overworking.

6. **Communicate Boundaries with Family and Friends:** Communicate your work hours and the importance of uninterrupted work time to family and friends. Setting clear boundaries with loved ones helps minimize distractions and interruptions during work hours.

7. **Limit Personal Activities during Work Hours:** Avoid engaging in personal activities during designated work hours. This includes refraining from personal phone calls, household chores, or personal errands that can disrupt your work focus.

8. **Use Digital Communication Wisely:** Set boundaries with digital communication tools, such as email and messaging apps. Avoid checking work emails or messages during personal time to prevent work-related stress from bleeding into your personal life.

9. **Establish a Sign-Off Ritual:** Create a sign-off ritual at the end of your workday to mark the transition from work to personal time. This can be as simple as shutting down your computer, closing your work

applications, or writing a to-do list for the next day.

10.   **Engage in Non-Work Activities:** Make time for non-work activities that you enjoy, such as hobbies, exercise, spending time with family, or pursuing personal interests. Engaging in these activities during personal time helps you recharge and maintain a healthy work-life balance.

Remember that maintaining work-life boundaries is a continuous process that requires self-discipline and commitment. By implementing these strategies and communicating your boundaries clearly with colleagues and family members, you can create a more balanced and fulfilling remote work experience.

The Impact of Remote Work on Urbanization and Real Estate Trends

The impact of remote work on urbanization and real estate trends has been significant and far-reaching. As more companies adopt remote work policies, and employees embrace the flexibility of working from anywhere, there have been noticeable shifts in population distribution, housing preferences, and real estate demands. Let's delve into the details of these impacts:

1. **Suburban and Rural Migration:** Remote work has led to a migration of workers from urban centers to suburban and rural areas. With the freedom to work from anywhere, many employees are choosing to move

to areas with lower costs of living, more space, and a quieter lifestyle. This shift has put pressure on suburban and rural real estate markets, driving up demand for properties in these areas.

2. Decentralization of Business Centers:

As remote work becomes more prevalent, businesses are reevaluating the need for large centralized office spaces in urban hubs. Instead of concentrating employees in one location, companies are embracing a distributed workforce, which reduces the demand for prime office spaces in city centers. This decentralization trend is likely to impact commercial real estate markets in urban areas.

3. Changes in Housing Preferences:

Remote work has altered housing preferences for both renters and homeowners. People are seeking homes with more space, home offices, and outdoor amenities. This has led to increased interest in single-family homes and properties with larger yards, which were traditionally less in demand in densely populated urban areas.

4. Impact on Housing Prices:

The shift in housing preferences and increased demand for properties in suburban and rural areas have led to price appreciation in these regions. On the other hand, some urban centers are experiencing a softening in housing prices as demand for city living declines. However, it's important to note that real estate trends can vary based on regional factors and market conditions.

5. Revitalization of Small Towns:

Remote work has contributed to the revitalization of small towns and previously overlooked regions.

Workers seeking a change of scenery and a lower cost of living are moving to small towns, injecting life and economic activity into these communities. This trend has the potential to rejuvenate local economies and create new opportunities in smaller urban areas.

6. **Impact on Commercial Real Estate:**
The increase in remote work has had a direct impact on the commercial real estate sector. Many companies are reconsidering their office space needs and opting for flexible office arrangements, such as co-working spaces or hybrid models that combine remote work with occasional in-office collaboration. This shift in demand for office space may lead to repurposing or adaptive reuse of commercial properties.

7. **Urban Revitalization Efforts:**
To attract residents and retain talent, some urban centers are investing in revitalization efforts. Urban planners are reimagining city spaces to offer more amenities, green spaces, and cultural attractions to cater to the changing needs and preferences of remote workers and urban dwellers.

8. **Impact on Transportation and Infrastructure:**
With fewer people commuting to offices daily, there may be changes in transportation and infrastructure needs. Reduced congestion and commuter traffic may require adjustments in public transportation services and road infrastructure planning.

9. **Focus on Digital Infrastructure:**
The growth of remote work has highlighted the importance of robust

digital infrastructure, including reliable internet connectivity. Governments and real estate developers may invest in improving digital infrastructure to support remote work capabilities in suburban and rural areas.

In conclusion, the impact of remote work on urbanization and real estate trends is multifaceted and dynamic. As remote work becomes more permanent and widespread, cities, real estate markets, and businesses are adjusting to accommodate the changing landscape of work and living preferences. The long-term effects will likely continue to evolve as societies adapt to the new era of remote work and embrace the opportunities it presents for both individuals and communities.

Remote Work and the Digital Skills Gap

Remote work has significantly influenced the digital skills gap, which refers to the disparity between the skills demanded by the job market, particularly in the digital realm, and the skills possessed by the workforce. The rapid transition to remote work has accelerated the need for digital skills, and organizations are increasingly seeking employees who can effectively navigate digital technologies and tools. Let's explore in detail how remote work has impacted the digital skills gap:

1. **Increased Demand for Digital Skills:**
   Remote work relies heavily on digital tools and technologies for communication, collaboration, and

productivity. As organizations shift to remote work models, there is a heightened demand for employees who can proficiently use digital communication platforms, project management software, cloud-based tools, and other remote work technologies.

2. Emphasis on Remote Collaboration and Digital Communication:

With remote work becoming the norm, the ability to collaborate effectively in virtual environments has become a crucial skill. Employees need to be adept at using video conferencing platforms, team chat applications, and other digital communication tools to interact with colleagues and clients remotely.

3. Need for Cybersecurity Awareness:

Remote work introduces new cybersecurity challenges, such as protecting sensitive data in home environments and recognizing phishing attempts in digital communication. Organizations require employees with a heightened awareness of cybersecurity best practices to mitigate risks and ensure data protection.

4. **Digital Literacy for Remote Productivity:**
   To maintain productivity in remote work settings, employees must possess digital literacy skills. This includes proficiency in using productivity software, file-sharing platforms, online document collaboration tools, and time management applications.

5. **Remote Training and Skill Development:**
   The shift to remote work has underscored the importance of ongoing training and skill development for employees.

Organizations are investing in remote training programs to upskill their workforce in digital competencies and bridge the digital skills gap.

6. **Impact on Hiring and Recruitment:**
Remote work has expanded the geographical scope of talent acquisition, allowing companies to hire employees from anywhere. However, this also means that job seekers must compete in a global talent pool, emphasizing the significance of possessing digital skills to stand out in remote job markets.

7. **Support for Digital Inclusion:**
Remote work highlights the importance of digital inclusion to ensure that all employees have access to necessary digital resources and skills. Organizations must consider the needs of employees who may face

digital barriers and provide support and training to promote equal opportunities for remote work.

8. Adaptation to Digital Transformation:

For businesses to thrive in a remote work environment, they must undergo digital transformation. This involves adopting digital tools, updating workflows, and redefining processes. The digital skills gap can hinder this transformation if employees lack the necessary skills to embrace digital change effectively.

9. Integration of Emerging Technologies:

Remote work has also accelerated the integration of emerging technologies, such as artificial intelligence, automation, and virtual reality, into work processes. Employees need to be equipped with the skills to work alongside these technologies and leverage their capabilities to enhance productivity.

In conclusion, remote work has magnified the importance of digital skills in the modern workforce. The rapid adoption of remote work technologies and the need for seamless collaboration in virtual environments have intensified the digital skills gap. To bridge this gap and succeed in remote work environments, organizations must prioritize digital skill development, offer remote training opportunities, and create a culture of continuous learning. Equipping the workforce with the necessary digital competencies will not only drive productivity in remote work settings but also prepare organizations for the digital future.

The Psychological and Social Implications of Remote Work

The widespread adoption of remote work has brought about various psychological and social implications for employees, teams, and organizations. While remote work offers flexibility and convenience, it also presents unique challenges that can impact well-being, team dynamics, and overall workplace culture. Let's explore in detail the psychological and social implications of remote work:

Psychological Implications:

1. **Isolation and Loneliness:** Remote work can lead to feelings of isolation and loneliness, as employees may miss

the social interactions and camaraderie of an office environment. The lack of face-to-face contact with colleagues can result in decreased morale and a sense of disconnection.

2. **Work-Life Boundaries:** The blurring of work and personal life in remote work setups can lead to difficulties in establishing clear boundaries between the two. Employees may struggle to disconnect from work, leading to burnout and reduced work-life balance.

3. **Autonomy and Empowerment:** On the positive side, remote work can foster a sense of autonomy and empowerment for employees. They have more control over their schedules and work environment, which can increase job satisfaction and motivation.

4. **Communication Challenges:**
Remote work can pose
communication challenges, such as
misinterpretation of messages,
difficulty in gauging nonverbal cues,
and potential delays in response time.
These challenges can lead to
misunderstandings and frustration
among team members.

5. **Performance Anxiety:** Some
employees may experience
performance anxiety in remote work
setups, fearing that their productivity
or performance may be judged solely
based on output, without the context
of face-to-face interactions and
presence.

6. **Impact on Mental Health:** Remote
work can impact mental health in
various ways. Employees may
experience increased stress due to
blurred boundaries, feelings of
isolation, and concerns about job

security. Employers need to be attentive to employees' mental well-being and provide appropriate support.

Social Implications:

1. **Team Cohesion and Collaboration:** Remote work can impact team dynamics and collaboration. Without in-person interactions, it may take more effort to build team cohesion and maintain a sense of camaraderie. Virtual team-building activities and regular team meetings can help bridge the gap.

2. **Trust and Communication:** Trust becomes critical in remote work setups. Team members and managers must trust that employees are working diligently even without direct supervision. Effective communication becomes the cornerstone of successful remote teams.

3. **Diversity and Inclusion:** Remote work has the potential to enhance diversity and inclusion by providing access to a broader talent pool and accommodating individuals with different needs and abilities. However, it also requires intentional efforts to create an inclusive remote work culture.

4. **Organizational Culture:** Remote work can influence organizational culture. Companies must adapt their culture to foster engagement, collaboration, and a sense of belonging among remote employees.

5. **Knowledge Sharing and Innovation:** Remote work can impact knowledge sharing and innovation. The spontaneous exchange of ideas and knowledge that occurs in physical workplaces may require intentional efforts in remote settings.

6. **Talent Acquisition and Retention:** Remote work expands

the geographical scope of talent acquisition. Companies that embrace remote work may attract and retain employees who value flexibility and work-life balance.

In conclusion, remote work has both positive and challenging psychological and social implications. While it can empower employees with autonomy and flexibility, it can also lead to feelings of isolation, communication challenges, and difficulties in maintaining work-life boundaries. To foster a positive remote work experience, organizations should prioritize employee well-being, promote effective communication and collaboration, and create a supportive and inclusive remote work culture. By addressing the psychological and social implications of remote work, companies can maximize the benefits of remote work arrangements and create a thriving and engaged remote workforce.

Remote Work and its Influence on Employee Engagement and Retention

Remote work has a significant influence on employee engagement and retention. When implemented effectively, remote work can positively impact employee satisfaction, motivation, and commitment to the organization. However, it also presents unique challenges that employers must address to maintain high levels of engagement and retention among remote employees. Let's explore in detail how remote work influences employee engagement and retention:

1. **Flexibility and Work-Life Balance:**
   Remote work offers employees greater flexibility in managing their work schedules and personal commitments. This flexibility can lead to improved

work-life balance, which is a crucial factor in employee satisfaction and retention. Employees who can better balance their work and personal lives are more likely to be engaged and committed to their jobs.

2. **Autonomy and Empowerment:** Remote work empowers employees by providing them with a greater sense of autonomy and ownership over their work. When employees have control over their work environment and schedules, they feel more trusted and valued by the organization. This increased autonomy can lead to higher levels of engagement and job satisfaction.

3. **Impact on Well-Being:** Remote work can positively impact employee well-being, especially for those who have long commutes or face challenges with traditional office settings. Remote work eliminates the

stress of daily commuting, which can lead to improved mental and physical well-being. Employees with better well-being are more likely to be engaged and committed to their roles.

4. **Communication and Collaboration:**
Remote work relies heavily on effective communication and collaboration tools. Organizations that prioritize seamless communication and encourage virtual collaboration create a sense of connectivity among remote employees. Regular check-ins, team meetings, and virtual social activities can foster a sense of belonging and engagement within remote teams.

5. **Challenges in Remote Work Engagement:**
While remote work offers numerous benefits, it also poses challenges for

employee engagement and retention. Remote employees may feel isolated, experience communication gaps, or struggle with work-life boundaries. Employers must proactively address these challenges to maintain high levels of engagement.

6. **Focus on Results and Outcomes:** Remote work emphasizes a results-oriented approach, focusing on what employees accomplish rather than their physical presence in the office. This can promote a culture of trust and performance-based evaluation, encouraging employees to be engaged and focused on achieving goals.

7. **Training and Development Opportunities:** To keep remote employees engaged and invested in their roles, organizations must provide ample

training and development opportunities. Remote employees should have access to resources that support their professional growth and skill development, enhancing their engagement and retention.

8. Recognition and Rewards: Recognizing and rewarding remote employees for their contributions and achievements is vital for maintaining engagement and fostering a positive work environment. Regular feedback and acknowledgment of their efforts can boost morale and motivation.

9. Inclusive Remote Culture: Creating an inclusive remote work culture is crucial for engagement and retention. Organizations should ensure that remote employees feel valued and included, despite physical distance. Encouraging team-building activities and celebrating remote team accomplishments can foster a sense of belonging.

10. **Career Growth and Advancement:**
Remote employees should have access to career growth opportunities within the organization. Employers must prioritize providing remote employees with a clear career path and avenues for advancement, as this plays a significant role in employee retention.

In conclusion, remote work can positively influence employee engagement and retention by offering flexibility, autonomy, and improved work-life balance. However, it also presents challenges that require proactive strategies and a focus on communication, collaboration, and well-being. By addressing these factors and fostering an inclusive and supportive remote work culture, organizations can maximize the benefits of remote work and create a motivated and committed remote workforce.

Overcoming the Loneliness and Isolation of Remote Work

Overcoming the loneliness and isolation of remote work is essential for maintaining well-being, productivity, and overall job satisfaction. Remote work can lead to feelings of isolation, especially when employees lack face-to-face interactions with colleagues. However, there are several strategies that individuals and organizations can implement to combat loneliness and foster a sense of connection and community in remote work environments:

1. **Maintain Regular Communication:**
   Regular communication is vital in remote work to stay connected with

colleagues and managers. Utilize video conferencing, team chat tools, and other communication platforms to have virtual face-to-face interactions and maintain a sense of camaraderie.

2. Schedule Virtual Social Activities:

Plan virtual social activities and team-building events to encourage informal interactions among remote team members. Virtual coffee breaks, online games, or virtual happy hours can help employees bond and build relationships outside of work tasks.

3. Participate in Online Communities:

Join online communities and forums related to your industry or interests. Engaging with like-minded professionals in these communities can provide a sense of belonging and connection, even when working remotely.

4. Establish a Remote Work Buddy System:

Implement a remote work buddy system where employees are paired with colleagues to check in on each other regularly. This can foster a sense of support and accountability in a remote work setup.

5. Create a Virtual Watercooler Space:

Set up a virtual watercooler space, such as a chat channel or virtual room, where employees can engage in informal conversations, share interests, and discuss non-work-related topics.

6. Attend Virtual Networking Events:

Participate in virtual conferences, webinars, and networking events to stay connected with industry peers and expand your professional network. These events provide opportunities to interact with others in your field, even from a distance.

7. Seek Support from Managers:

Managers should be proactive in addressing the well-being of remote employees. Regular check-ins, one-on-one meetings, and open communication channels can create a supportive environment and help employees feel less isolated.

8. Create a Comfortable Home Workspace:

Designate a dedicated and comfortable workspace in your home that is conducive to productivity. A well-designed home office can help establish a mental boundary between work and personal life, reducing feelings of isolation during off-hours.

9. Establish Work-Life Boundaries:

Set clear work-life boundaries to prevent work from encroaching on personal time. Allocate specific times for work and leisure activities, and avoid checking work emails or messages outside of designated work hours.

10. Consider Coworking Spaces (If Safe and Feasible):

If possible and safe, consider using coworking spaces occasionally to have a change of scenery and interact with other professionals in person. Coworking spaces can provide a sense of community and reduce feelings of isolation.

In conclusion, overcoming the loneliness and isolation of remote work requires intentional efforts from both individuals and organizations. Regular communication, virtual social activities, and networking opportunities can help remote employees build connections and combat feelings of isolation. Establishing supportive remote work practices and maintaining a healthy work-life balance are essential for fostering a positive remote work experience and ensuring employee well-being.

Remote Work and the Future of Commuting and Transportation

Remote work has the potential to transform the future of commuting and transportation in significant ways. As more companies adopt remote work policies and employees embrace the flexibility of working from home or other remote locations, commuting patterns and transportation systems are likely to experience notable changes. Let's explore in detail how remote work can impact the future of commuting and transportation:

1. **Reduced Traffic Congestion:** One of the most evident impacts of remote work is the reduction in traffic congestion during peak commuting

hours. With fewer people commuting to offices daily, rush-hour traffic is likely to decrease, leading to smoother and faster transportation flows in urban areas.

2. Shift in Public Transportation Demand:

Remote work may influence the demand for public transportation. While some individuals may still rely on public transit for occasional in-person meetings or workdays, the overall demand for daily commutes may decrease, affecting public transportation revenues and operations.

3. Impact on Public Transit Infrastructure:

With reduced demand for daily commuting, governments and public transit agencies may need to reassess their investments in public transit infrastructure. They may prioritize other transportation projects or adapt existing systems to better serve changing transportation needs.

4. Focus on Last-Mile Transportation:

As remote work becomes more prevalent, there may be increased emphasis on last-mile transportation solutions. Companies and cities may invest in bike-sharing programs, electric scooters, and micro-mobility options to facilitate shorter trips between home and local amenities.

5. Repurposing Office Spaces and Parking Facilities:

With more employees working remotely, some companies may choose to downsize their physical office spaces or shift to flexible office arrangements. This could lead to the repurposing of office buildings and associated parking facilities for other community uses or alternative businesses.

6. Regional Economic Impacts:

Remote work can influence economic activity in different regions. If employees no longer need to live close to urban centers for work, suburban and rural areas may experience an increase in economic activity as remote workers move to these regions.

7. Impact on Greenhouse Gas Emissions:

The reduction in commuting due to remote work can lead to a decrease in greenhouse gas emissions associated with transportation. Fewer cars on the roads during peak hours can contribute to improved air quality and environmental sustainability.

8. Changes in Transportation Policy:

The shift towards remote work may prompt governments to reevaluate transportation policies. Transportation plans and funding allocations may be adjusted to align with changing commuting patterns and the evolving needs of the workforce.

9. Telecommuting Incentives and Regulations:

To support remote work and encourage businesses to adopt flexible work arrangements, governments may introduce telecommuting incentives or regulations that offer tax benefits or other perks for companies that implement remote work policies.

10. Hybrid Transportation Models:

As remote work becomes more common, some employees may opt for hybrid transportation models, combining remote work with occasional visits to the office. This could lead to a shift towards flexible commuting options, such as part-time public transit passes or ride-sharing services.

In conclusion, remote work has the potential to reshape commuting and transportation in the future. It can lead to reduced traffic congestion, changes in public transit demand, and a focus on last-mile transportation solutions. The impact of remote work on commuting patterns will likely vary by region, and governments and transportation agencies will need to adapt to the evolving needs of the workforce. The potential benefits, such as reduced greenhouse gas emissions and improved work-life balance for employees, make remote work an influential factor in shaping the future of commuting and transportation.

The Emergence of Virtual Reality and Augmented Reality in Remote Workspaces

The emergence of virtual reality (VR) and augmented reality (AR) in remote workspaces is revolutionizing the way remote teams collaborate, communicate, and interact. These immersive technologies offer new possibilities for creating a virtual office environment and enhancing remote work experiences. Let's delve into the details of how VR and AR are transforming remote workspaces:

1. **Virtual Meetings and Collaboration:**
   VR and AR enable remote teams to hold virtual meetings and collaborate

in shared virtual spaces. Instead of traditional video conferencing, participants can join interactive virtual meeting rooms, where they appear as avatars in a 3D environment. This fosters a sense of presence and allows for more natural interactions, as participants can use gestures and body language just like in real-life meetings.

2. **Virtual Workspaces and Offices:** VR technology allows organizations to create virtual workspaces and offices, where remote employees can work together as if they were physically co-located. These virtual environments can be customized to mimic a traditional office layout or designed to be more innovative and immersive, depending on the organization's needs.

3. Enhanced Training and Onboarding:

AR and VR offer powerful tools for employee training and onboarding in remote work settings. Through AR, employees can access real-time information and guidance while performing tasks. VR simulations can be used for immersive training experiences, allowing employees to practice skills and scenarios in a risk-free environment.

4. Virtual Whiteboarding and Brainstorming:

AR and VR technologies enable teams to conduct virtual brainstorming sessions and whiteboarding activities. Remote team members can collaborate on a shared virtual canvas, allowing for real-time ideation and creative problem-solving.

5. Remote Technical Support:

AR can be utilized for remote technical support, where experts can provide remote guidance and assistance to employees on-site. Through AR-enabled devices, employees can receive visual instructions and annotations, simplifying complex tasks.

6. **Virtual Social Events and Team-Building Activities:** VR and AR offer opportunities for virtual social events and team-building activities, helping remote teams strengthen their bonds and sense of camaraderie. Virtual team-building games, workshops, and events can be organized to boost team morale and engagement.

7. **Remote Product Demonstrations:** In industries that require product demonstrations, AR can be used to provide remote customers with interactive, 3D product presentations. This enhances the customer

experience and allows for better visualization of products in real-world environments.

8. Remote Site Inspections and Tours:

In fields such as architecture, construction, and real estate, AR and VR can facilitate remote site inspections and virtual tours. Clients and stakeholders can remotely explore construction sites or properties using AR overlays or VR simulations.

9. Overcoming Distance Barriers:

By introducing VR and AR in remote workspaces, organizations can help employees feel more connected despite physical distances. The sense of presence and interactivity in virtual environments can bridge the gap between team members scattered across different locations.

10. **Data Visualization and Decision-Making:**
AR and VR can aid in data visualization, allowing remote teams to better understand complex datasets and make data-driven decisions collaboratively. Visualizing data in immersive environments can lead to more informed discussions and insights.

In conclusion, the integration of virtual reality and augmented reality in remote workspaces is revolutionizing the way remote teams collaborate, train, and conduct business. These technologies offer new possibilities for creating virtual meeting spaces, virtual work environments, and enhancing team interactions. As these technologies continue to advance, their applications in remote work are expected to expand, further transforming the future of remote workspaces.

Remote Work and the Rise of Co-working Spaces

Remote work has played a significant role in the rise of co-working spaces, which are shared workspaces that individuals and businesses can rent on a short-term basis. As remote work becomes more prevalent, the demand for flexible and collaborative work environments has increased, leading to the proliferation of co-working spaces worldwide. Let's explore in detail how remote work has contributed to the rise of co-working spaces:

1. **Flexibility for Remote Workers:** Co-working spaces offer remote workers the flexibility to work from a professional and well-equipped workspace without committing to a long-term lease. This flexibility is

especially appealing to freelancers, entrepreneurs, and remote employees who seek a change of scenery from their home offices.

2. **Amenities and Infrastructure:** Co-working spaces provide essential amenities and infrastructure, such as high-speed internet, meeting rooms, printing facilities, and communal areas. These amenities create a productive work environment for remote workers and eliminate the need for them to set up their own workspaces.

3. **Collaboration and Networking Opportunities:** One of the primary attractions of co-working spaces is the opportunity for collaboration and networking. Co-working environments bring together individuals from diverse industries and backgrounds, fostering connections, idea-sharing, and potential collaborations.

4. **Supportive Community:**

Working remotely can sometimes lead to feelings of isolation. Co-working spaces offer a supportive community of like-minded individuals who share similar work experiences and challenges. This sense of community can combat loneliness and enhance well-being for remote workers.

5. Professional Image:

For freelancers and independent professionals, using a co-working space can enhance their professional image. It provides a more credible and professional setting for meetings with clients and partners compared to meeting in coffee shops or at home.

6. Cost-Effective Solution:

For startups and small businesses, co-working spaces offer a cost-effective alternative to leasing traditional office spaces. Co-working memberships typically include utilities and other overhead costs, making it an economical choice for those on a tight budget.

7. Expansion of Remote Work Policies:

As more companies embrace remote work policies, employees may seek co-working spaces as a way to have a dedicated workspace outside of their homes. Employers may also subsidize coworking memberships to support remote employees' productivity and well-being.

8. Urban Revitalization:

The rise of co-working spaces has contributed to the revitalization of urban areas. By converting underutilized or vacant spaces into co-working hubs, these spaces can attract remote workers and entrepreneurs, boosting foot traffic and local economies.

9. Adaptation to Changing Work Trends:

The growth of co-working spaces reflects a broader trend of changing work patterns and the shift towards more flexible work arrangements. Co-working spaces are an adaptive response to the evolving needs of the modern workforce.

10.   Specialized Co-working Spaces:

Co-working spaces have diversified to cater to specific industries and niches. Some co-working spaces are tailored to support tech startups, creative professionals, or social impact organizations, creating tailored environments for different work needs.

In conclusion, remote work has been a driving force behind the rise of co-working spaces. The demand for flexible and collaborative workspaces has grown as more individuals and businesses embrace remote work arrangements. Co-working spaces offer a wide range of benefits, including flexibility, amenities, networking opportunities, and a supportive community. As remote work continues to shape the future of work, co-working spaces are expected to remain a popular and essential component of the modern work landscape.

Remote Work and its Effect on Corporate Hierarchies and Organizational Structures

---

Remote work has a profound effect on corporate hierarchies and organizational structures, reshaping the way companies operate, communicate, and make decisions. The shift to remote work introduces new challenges and opportunities for organizations to adapt their structures and leadership styles to accommodate a distributed workforce. Let's explore in detail how remote work impacts corporate hierarchies and organizational structures:

1. **Flattening of Hierarchies:**
   Remote work often fosters a more egalitarian work environment, as

physical distance is reduced, and employees at all levels can interact more directly. With fewer physical barriers, the traditional top-down hierarchical structure may become less rigid, promoting a more open and collaborative workplace.

2. Decentralization of Decision-Making:

Remote work allows organizations to distribute decision-making authority more widely. Empowering remote employees to make decisions in their areas of expertise can lead to quicker problem-solving and increased autonomy.

3. Emphasis on Results-Based Management:

In a remote work setting, the focus shifts from monitoring employees' hours worked to evaluating their output and results. This results-based management approach can foster a culture of accountability and trust, rather than relying solely on direct supervision.

4. **Digital Communication and Collaboration Tools:**
   Remote work relies heavily on digital communication and collaboration tools. Organizations adopt technologies like video conferencing, project management software, and team chat platforms to facilitate seamless communication and maintain productivity across distributed teams.

5. **Redefined Roles and Skill Sets:**
   As remote work requires adaptability and self-reliance, employees' roles may evolve to include a broader range of responsibilities. Cross-functional collaboration and continuous learning

become essential components of remote work skill sets.

6. Focus on Performance Metrics:
Remote work necessitates the establishment of clear performance metrics to measure productivity and contribution. Organizations may develop new key performance indicators (KPIs) to assess remote employees' performance effectively.

7. Virtual Leadership and Management:
Managers must adapt their leadership styles to effectively manage remote teams. Virtual leadership involves setting clear expectations, providing support and feedback, and fostering a positive team culture in a remote work environment.

8. Reimagined Office Spaces:

With remote work becoming more prevalent, some companies may reconsider their physical offices as collaborative hubs for occasional in-person interactions.

9. Focus on Employee Engagement and Well-Being:

Remote work highlights the importance of employee engagement and well-being. Organizations must prioritize initiatives to support remote employees, such as virtual team-building activities, well-being resources, and opportunities for professional development.

10. Emphasis on Inclusive Communication:

Organizations need to prioritize inclusive communication practices to ensure that remote employees feel connected and engaged. This involves sharing information transparently, offering equal opportunities for participation, and ensuring that remote employees are not excluded from important discussions.

In conclusion, remote work has a transformative effect on corporate hierarchies and organizational structures. Flattening of hierarchies, decentralization of decision-making, and results-based management are among the changes brought about by remote work. Virtual leadership, digital communication tools, and an emphasis on employee well-being become critical components of successful remote work structures. Organizations that adapt and embrace these changes can create a more agile, inclusive, and resilient workforce capable of thriving in a remote work environment.

Managing Remote Teams:

Best Practices and Strategies for Success

Managing remote teams effectively requires a set of best practices and strategies to ensure communication, collaboration, and productivity. Remote work introduces unique challenges that demand a proactive approach from managers to support their team members and foster a positive remote work culture. Let's explore in detail the best practices and strategies for successfully managing remote teams:

1. **Clear Communication Guidelines:**
   Establish clear communication guidelines and expectations for remote team members. Define preferred communication channels, response times, and guidelines for

asynchronous communication to ensure everyone stays informed and connected.

2. Emphasize Goal Setting and Expectations:

Set clear performance goals and expectations for remote team members. This provides a sense of direction and accountability, as well as a framework for evaluating performance in a remote work environment.

3. Adopt Collaboration and Productivity Tools:

Leverage collaboration and productivity tools to facilitate remote teamwork. Utilize video conferencing platforms, project management tools, team chat applications, and file-sharing platforms to support seamless collaboration and communication.

4. **Regular Check-Ins and One-on-Ones:**
   Schedule regular check-in meetings and one-on-one sessions with remote team members. These meetings provide opportunities to discuss progress, address challenges, and provide support and feedback on individual performance.

5. **Virtual Team-Building Activities:**
   Organize virtual team-building activities and social events to foster team cohesion and a sense of belonging. These activities can include virtual games, online workshops, or informal team get-togethers.

6. **Support Work-Life Balance:**
   Encourage a healthy work-life balance among remote team members. Be mindful of their working hours and provide flexibility to accommodate personal commitments. Avoid

expecting immediate responses outside of regular working hours.

7. Prioritize Inclusivity and Diversity:

Promote inclusivity and diversity in remote teams. Ensure that remote team members have equal access to opportunities, resources, and information to foster a sense of belonging and equality.

8. Recognize and Celebrate Achievements:

Acknowledge and celebrate the accomplishments of remote team members. Recognizing their efforts and contributions boosts morale and motivation, even from a distance.

9. Invest in Remote Training and Skill Development:

Provide opportunities for remote team members to develop new skills and enhance their professional growth. Remote training programs and workshops can help keep the team up-to-date with industry trends and best practices.

10. Foster a Positive Remote Work Culture:

Create a positive remote work culture that values trust, open communication, and mutual support. Encourage team members to share ideas, feedback, and concerns openly, creating an environment of psychological safety.

11. Address Conflict and Communication Issues Promptly:

If conflicts or communication issues arise among team members, address them promptly and directly. Encourage open and respectful communication to resolve issues and maintain team cohesion.

12.   Lead by Example:
As a remote team manager, lead by example in embracing remote work practices and demonstrating a strong work ethic. Show that you are accessible, responsive, and committed to supporting your team's success.

In conclusion, successfully managing remote teams requires a thoughtful approach that prioritizes communication, collaboration, and employee well-being. By setting clear expectations, adopting the right tools, and fostering a positive remote work culture, managers can build a cohesive and productive remote team. Regular check-ins, virtual team-building activities, and recognition of achievements contribute to team morale and motivation. Embracing inclusivity, promoting work-life balance, and investing in employee growth are essential components of managing remote teams effectively.

Remote Work and the Reshaping of Career Paths and Job Opportunities.

Remote work has significantly reshaped career paths and job opportunities for professionals across various industries. The shift to remote work has opened up new possibilities and transformed traditional work dynamics, creating a more flexible and accessible job market. Let's explore in detail how remote work has influenced career paths and job opportunities:

1. **Access to Global Job Market:** Remote work allows individuals to apply for job opportunities beyond their geographical location. Job seekers can pursue positions with companies located anywhere in the

world, providing access to a more extensive and diverse job market.

2. Remote Job Opportunities:

The rise of remote work has led to the creation of remote-specific job opportunities. Companies are now hiring remote employees for various roles that can be performed from any location, such as remote customer support, virtual assistants, remote software development, and digital marketing roles.

3. Career Advancement and Skill Development:

Remote work often emphasizes performance-based evaluation and outcome-driven results. This can create opportunities for career advancement based on individual merit and skill development rather than traditional tenure-based promotions.

4. Rise of Freelancing and Gig Economy:

Remote work has contributed to the growth of the freelance and gig economy. Many professionals choose to work as freelancers or independent contractors, offering their services to multiple clients and embracing a flexible work lifestyle.

5. Work-Life Integration:

Remote work allows professionals to integrate work into their lives more seamlessly. This can lead to the exploration of non-traditional career paths, such as pursuing side projects, starting their own businesses, or taking on remote part-time work while managing other personal commitments.

6. Demand for Remote-Specific Skills:

With the increased adoption of remote work, certain skills have become more valuable in the job market. Skills such as remote collaboration, digital communication, and adaptability to remote tools and technologies are highly sought after by employers.

7. **Remote Leadership Opportunities:**
Remote work has expanded leadership opportunities for individuals who can effectively manage and lead remote teams. Remote managers need to possess strong communication and remote leadership skills to guide and support their distributed teams effectively.

8. **Impact on Traditional Industries:**
Remote work has also influenced traditional industries by requiring them to adapt to remote work practices. Companies that previously relied on physical presence are now exploring remote work options,

creating new job opportunities within those industries.

9. Workforce Demographics and Diversity:

Remote work has the potential to attract a more diverse workforce, including individuals with disabilities, caregivers, and those living in remote or rural areas. This can lead to a more inclusive and diverse job market.

10. Emphasis on Soft Skills:

Remote work places a greater emphasis on soft skills, such as communication, self-discipline, and time management. Job seekers and professionals must showcase their remote work readiness and ability to thrive in a virtual work environment.

In conclusion, remote work has reshaped career paths and job opportunities by expanding the global job market, creating remote-specific roles, and fostering a flexible work culture. Professionals now have access to a broader range of job opportunities, and remote work has influenced the way individuals navigate their careers. The rise of remote work has also accelerated the growth of the freelance and gig economy, emphasizing the importance of remote-specific skills and soft skills in the modern job market. As remote work continues to evolve, professionals must adapt their skill sets and career strategies to capitalize on the changing job landscape.